Our
Values

# FAIR TRADE & GLOBAL ECONOMY

by

## Charlie Ogden

©2018
**Book Life**
**King's Lynn**
**Norfolk PE30 4LS**

**ISBN:** 978-1-78637-233-8

**Written by:**
Charlie Ogden

**Edited by:**
Kirsty Holmes

**Designed by:**
Danielle Jones

# CONTENTS

Words that look like **this** can be can be found in the glossary on page 31.

# WHAT IS AN ECONOMY?

The word 'economy' is used to talk about the ways that a **country** makes and spends money. A country's economy is made up of the **goods** and **services** that the people in the country use, the goods and services the people produce and the amount of money the people spend on these goods and services.

WORKING OUT A COUNTRY'S ECONOMY IS VERY COMPLICATED AND IT INVOLVES COLLECTING A HUGE AMOUNT OF INFORMATION.

Countries are often said to have either a weak economy or a strong economy. Countries with weak economies are often poor and their **citizens** have to be careful with their money. Countries with strong economies usually make a lot of money and their citizens are able to spend a lot on goods and services. Most of the time, these places also have good schools, roads and hospitals. However, a country's economy can go from strong to weak very quickly and when this happens, it usually makes life for its citizens much harder.

# ECONOMIES AND TRADING

People in different countries often sell different goods and services to one another. This is called trading. Some countries trade a lot more than others, but every country trades with at least some other countries. Many people trade goods because they can only get certain products from other countries.

For example, the United Kingdom imports all of its coffee from countries in South America and Asia. This is because coffee beans, which are used to make coffee, cannot grow in the United Kingdom. To get coffee, **organisations** in the United Kingdom have to trade with people in countries where coffee beans can grow.

This hillside in Colombia, South America, is covered in coffee plants.

GOODS AND SERVICES BOUGHT FROM OTHER COUNTRIES ARE CALLED IMPORTS. GOODS AND SERVICES SOLD TO OTHER COUNTRIES ARE CALLED EXPORTS.

## THE GLOBAL ECONOMY

Different countries and their economies are linked together by the trading of goods and services. Because of this, many people say that there is now a global economy. The global economy is a way of looking at the complicated relationships between the economies of different countries. It is also used to talk about how one country's economy can affect another country's economy.

# WHY IS THERE A GLOBAL ECONOMY?

For thousands of years, people have talked about the economies of cities and countries. However, it is only in the last few decades that people have started to talk about the economy of the entire world. Why is this the case?

THE STEEL CONTAINERS USED ON CONTAINER SHIPS ARE ALL EXACTLY THE SAME SIZE. ALL THE SHIPS, TRAINS AND TRUCKS IN THE WORLD CARRY JUST THIS ONE SIZE OF CONTAINER. THIS MAKES IT EASY TO TRANSPORT GOODS TO ALMOST ANYWHERE.

In the last 100 years, lots of technology has been created that has made trading goods between countries easy. Today, we have container ships that can **transport** huge amounts of goods between different **ports** as well as aeroplanes and trucks that can take goods across land. Nowadays, we also have telephones and computers, which allow people on different sides of the planet to work together. This technology has made global trade possible, so now we have a global economy.

New technology has also made it much cheaper to transport goods. This is important. In the past, even if an organisation in France could arrange to buy something, such as planks of wood, from a country on the other side of the world, it would cost a lot of money to transport the wood back to France. Now that transporting goods is not as expensive, organisations are able to buy their goods from the cheapest place possible.

Canada exports more wood than any other country in the world.

WITHOUT THE COMPUTER TECHNOLOGY WE HAVE TODAY, IT WOULD BE DIFFICULT FOR ORGANISATIONS TO **employ** PEOPLE IN OTHER COUNTRIES.

However, it is not only goods that can be cheaper in other countries. Many organisations also hire people in other countries because they are cheaper to **employ** than people from their own country.

For example, many people in India are employed by companies from the United States of America. This is because they do not cost as much to employ and they can do their jobs from the other side of the world.

# EFFECTS OF THE
# GLOBAL ECONOMY

In the global economy, it is far more common for **more economically developed** (MED) **countries** with lots of money, such as the United States of America, China or Germany, to import goods and services from **less economically developed** (LED) **countries**, such as Vietnam or Costa Rica. Organisations in MED countries often import a wide range of goods – mainly food, building materials and fuel – from different countries around the world. On the other hand, many organisations in LED countries do not have the money to buy goods from countries that are far away.

BELGIUM, A SMALL, MED COUNTRY IN EUROPE, DOESN'T HAVE THE resources TO PROVIDE LOTS OF DIFFERENT FOODS FOR ITS CITIZENS. INSTEAD, ORGANISATIONS IN BELGIUM IMPORT LOTS OF FOOD FROM LED COUNTRIES, SUCH AS THAILAND.

When you look at what jobs people have in different countries, you can see the effect that the global economy has had on the world. As it is cheap for MED countries to import food, these countries often have a smaller amount of citizens working in **agriculture**. On the other hand, as LED countries can sometimes make lots of money from exporting food to other countries, these countries often have a larger amount of citizens working in agriculture. For example, 40% of people in Thailand work in agriculture-related jobs, whereas only around 1% of people in Belgium do.

The global economy has been shaped by the fact that organisations and people want to make money. Organisations in MED countries buy goods from other countries because they are cheap and they can sell the goods for more money. People in LED countries sell their services to organisations in other countries because they want to make money. However, this desire to buy things cheaply and make lots of money has sometimes led to people in LED countries getting **exploited** by organisations in wealthy countries.

People in LED countries who work in agriculture are often only paid a small amount of money for the food they produce. In many cases, this food goes on to be sold for lots of money in MED countries. Foods such as fruit, chocolate and coffee can be some of the most expensive items in the supermarket. However, the farmers in Africa, Asia and South America who spend their grow the plants to produce these foods often only get a tiny portion of the money made from selling them.

This is a banana plantation in India. A plantation is a large farm where crops are grown in order to be sold to make money.

# WHAT IS FAIR TRADE?

'Fair trade' is the idea that global trading should be fair and **equal**. Many MED countries have laws to make sure that people in their country trade goods and services in a fair and equal way. However, there are few **international** trading laws to protect people in LED countries who trade with organisations in MED countries. Fair trade is the idea that rules should be put in place to protect LED countries and their citizens.

Fair trade is most concerned with goods such as coffee beans, fruit, cocoa, cotton, wine, sugar, flowers and gold. These goods are usually exported from LED countries to wealthy MED countries and the people who produce them are often not treated equally or paid a fair **wage**.

LAWS ARE RULES THAT ARE MEANT TO PROTECT PEOPLE AND THEY MUST BE FOLLOWED BY EVERYONE IN A CERTAIN AREA. INTERNATIONAL LAWS ARE RULES THAT EVERYONE IN THE WORLD MUST FOLLOW.

Fair trade is the idea that a good portion of the money made from selling a food, such as a banana, should be given to the farmer who grew it. Paying these workers more money gives them a fairer share of the money made from their bananas and also means that they can buy better farming equipment. This should help the farmers to grow bananas more easily in the future, meaning they will get even more money and people around the world can enjoy more bananas.

Supporters of fair trade also believe in using sustainable farming methods. These are ways of farming that do not badly affect the environment. A non-sustainable farming method would be one that affected the environment badly. For example, cutting down areas of forest to make room for more fields is a non-sustainable farming method.

# FAIR TRADE AND THE GLOBAL ECONOMY

Supporters of fair trade believe that by paying farmers a fair amount for their work, they will be able to use sustainable farming methods and everyone will be better off. This is because sustainable farming methods make sure that farms around the world continue producing **crops** in the future. Such farming methods should also help to protect the environment and reduce the impact that farming has on animals and plants.

Many non-sustainable methods are cheap, but can be dangerous in the long-term. For example, chemicals known as pesticides are often sprayed onto fields to kill insects that try to damage crops. However, some of these chemicals can **pollute** the soil and make it more difficult for crops to grow in the future.

Pesticides are cheap and effective, but using them can damage the environment and make farming more difficult in the future. By paying farmers more for their crops, they will be able to afford to use sustainable farming methods.

Many people believe that fair trade rules will help the global economy. This is because all countries are linked by trade, meaning that putting more money into one country can also help strengthen the economies of other countries. As more and more developing countries start to have strong economies, the global economy will become stronger as well.

By giving the vegetable farmers in a developing country more money for their work, more money is put into that country's economy. This will help the country's economy to become stronger and could help organisations in the country to become more involved in fair trading. They could start to grow even more vegetables than before using better, more expensive farming methods, helping them to trade with organisations all over the world. All this trading is likely to help to make the global economy stronger.

By looking at what can happen when farmers are exploited by organisations in more economically developed countries, it is easy to see why fair trade is important.

Organisations wanting to buy a certain crop, such as sugar cane, could buy it from a number of different farms in a number of different countries. With no fair trade rules in place, the organisation will try to buy the sugar cane for as little as possible. The organisation can ask a farm to sell its sugar cane for a very low price. The farm doesn't have to agree.

However, if the farm asks for more money, the organisation might go to a different farm for cheaper sugar cane. If this happens, it is possible that no other organisation will come to the farm and the sugar cane will never be sold. If they are scared this might happen, the farm will sell its sugar cane for a low price.

BRAZIL GROWS TWICE AS MUCH SUGAR CANE AS ANY OTHER COUNTRY. MOST OF THIS SUGAR CANE IS USED TO MAKE SUGAR WHICH GETS EXPORTED TO OTHER COUNTRIES.

This plantation in Thailand is growing sugar cane. Sugar cane is one of the main plants that is used to make sugar.

If the sugar cane farm wasn't paid enough for its crops, it would need to look for other ways to make enough money to pay its farmers. To make room to grow even more crops, large areas of grassland or forest might get cleared.

This would destroy **habitats**, but would mean the farmers could make more money. Farmers might start using harmful pesticides. This could damage the soil and harm nearby habitats, but it would help the farm to get more sugar cane out of the fields it already has.

If these ideas were not possible, the farmers might need to do other things to make more money from their crops. The farmers may get paid so little that they cannot support their families, leaving them without proper homes or enough food to eat. Instead, the farmers may have to work long hours in dangerous conditions just to get enough money for food. If this isn't enough, the farm might start employing children to work in the sugar cane fields. These options are very unfair and many people believe they go against **human rights**. If fair trade laws are put in place, many people believe that a sugar cane farm would not be put in this position and its farmers and the environment would be protected from harm.

# ECONOMIES AROUND THE WORLD

## STRONG ECONOMIES

There are many things that can help to make a country's economy strong and lots of the strongest economies in the world are very different from one another. Some countries make money from trading lots of different goods, but others export only a few goods. Norway has one of the strongest economies in the world. It exports a range of different goods and has citizens employed in a range of different jobs.

A large portion of the money coming into Norway's economy comes from exporting **fossil fuels**. Companies in Norway sell fossil fuels around the world. Norway also has a long coastline. Because of this, Norway also exports a lot of fish, such as herring, cod and halibut. Another resource that organisations in Norway can use is the wood from forests, which cover around one third of the country. Lots of organisations in Norway sell the wood from the trees to other countries, which brings money into the Norwegian economy.

Norway

This is Oslo, the **capital city** of Norway.

While most countries with strong economies export lots of different goods, there are some countries that maintain a strong economy by exporting only a few goods. One such country is Qatar, which is a tiny country in the Middle East. Despite being so small, Qatar exports more fossil fuels than almost any other country in the world and this brings lots of money into the country's economy.

Qatar

This is Doha, the capital city of Qatar.

NATURAL GAS IS A TYPE OF FOSSIL FUEL AND IT IS FOUND DEEP UNDERGROUND. MORE NATURAL GAS IS MINED OUT OF THE GROUND IN QATAR THAN IN CHINA, A COUNTRY OVER 800 TIMES LARGER.

Qatar doesn't have a range of different resources that organisations in the country can easily export to other countries. While Norway also has lots of wood and fish that it can easily export, Qatar only has fossil fuels. Because of this, exporting fossil fuels makes up well over half of the money that comes into Qatar's economy. Despite this, Qatar is a very wealthy country and its citizens are able to buy imported goods from all over the world. This shows that, in some cases, it is possible to have a strong economy in a country that only has a few natural resources.

# WEAK ECONOMIES

Like with strong economies, there is more than one thing that can cause an economy to become weak or prevent it from becoming stronger. However, one thing that often leads to a country's economy being weak is lack of resources. When a country doesn't have **fertile** soil where crops can grow, water where people can catch fish or forests where people can collect wood, it often ends up having a weak economy. Burundi, which doesn't have many natural resources, has one of the weakest economies in the world.

This is Bujumbura, the capital city of Burundi.

Burundi

Burundi is a landlocked country, meaning that it doesn't have a coastline or access to the sea. This makes trading difficult for organisations in Burundi and means that they can't catch fish from the sea. Burundi also does not have large forests and much of its soil is not suitable for farming. This is partly because the country is covered by mountains, which are bad places to grow trees and crops. Because of the lack of resources in Burundi, 70% of its citizens work in agriculture and many of these people are only just able to grow enough food for themselves and their families. With very few goods being exported from Burundi, little money comes into Burundi's economy from other countries.

However, some counties have a weak economy for other reasons. One such country is Nepal. While Nepal faces many of the same problems as Burundi, such as being landlocked and having a lot of space taken up by mountains, many people believe that its economy struggles for other reasons. In the last **century**, the **government** in Nepal has changed a lot. This has made it difficult for the country's economy to become stronger, which has affected the lives of the people who live in Nepal.

Nepal

This is Kathmandu, the capital city of Nepal.

Up until 1951, the king of Nepal kept the country **isolated** from the outside world. This meant that it did not trade with other countries and very few people from outside Nepal were allowed to enter the country. This stopped Nepal from keeping up with modern technology and left the country with poor schools, hospitals and roads.

While the government in Nepal has made a lot of progress since 1951, other troubles have stopped Nepal's economy from becoming stronger. Today, Nepali citizens who work in other countries send lots of money back home to their families. This money makes up for a large portion of the money coming into Nepal's economy.

# FAIR TRADE AND THE GLOBAL ECONOMY TODAY

## THE GLOBAL ECONOMY

Today, every country in the world trades goods and services with other countries. Most countries need the things they import from other countries to give their citizens a range of goods and services to enjoy. Countries, especially small countries, also rely on the goods they import to provide their citizens with enough food.

This map shows the main types of goods that are exported from each country.

- ◼ Food/Drink
- ◼ Metals/Materials
- ◼ Wood Products
- ◼ Oil
- ◼ Textile/Apparel
- ◼ Machinery/Transportation
- ◼ Electronics
- ◼ Other

The money each country makes from exporting goods can often affect the lives of its citizens. By exporting goods, a country brings money into its economy. In most cases, this helps to strengthen the economy and makes life better for the citizens in that country. If a country makes less money than expected from exporting its goods, it can weaken the country's economy and make life harder for its citizens. As every country's economy is affected by international trading and every person is affected by their country's economy, it is easy to see how the world truly does have a global economy. Every person is part of it and every person can be affected by it.

People whose jobs are to do with the trading of goods and services between countries are part of the global workforce. Fruit farmers in LED countries are part of the global workforce because their fruit gets exported. Miners, factory workers and fishers are also part of the global workforce, as the goods they produce or collect often get exported to other countries.

People who are employed by organisations in other countries are part of the global workforce as well. In 1980, the global workforce was made up of around 1.2 billion people. Today, around 3 billion people – nearly half of the world's population – are part of the global workforce. Without international trading and the global economy, many of these jobs wouldn't exist.

All of these people are part of the global workforce.

We can see how much international trading happens just by looking at the different foods that people can buy in their local shop. In a normal Australian supermarket, people can buy tuna from Thailand, apple sauce from Belgium, cherries from Hungary, raspberries from Chile and sultanas from South Africa. Today, five different foods farmed in five different continents can all end up on the same shelf in a supermarket.

# FAIR TRADE

Over the last few decades, as the global workforce has increased and countries have begun trading more goods and services with one another, fair trade has become even more important. Today, there are lots of organisations that work to support fair trade and protect the human rights of the global workforce. However, there are many people who believe that more needs to be done.

Fairtrade International is one of the largest fair trade organisations in the world. It is a non-profit organisation, meaning that all the money it makes is used to help support fair trade. Fairtrade International looks into different organisations that trade goods to see if their workers are getting a fair wage and are working in safe conditions. If either of these things aren't up the Fairtrade Standards, then the organisation helps to get the workers more money and safer working conditions.

# THE FAIRTRADE STANDARDS

The Fairtrade Standards are a set of **criteria** that every trade organisation should meet. The standards were made by Fairtrade International and they aim to help producers in the poorest countries in the world. Producers are the people who grow, mine or make goods.

The main aims of the Fairtrade Standards are:

- To make sure that producers are paid enough live well.
- To make sure that producers are able to use sustainable farming methods.
- To help producers have more control over who they trade with.
- To ensure that trading goods doesn't badly affect the communities, economies or environments where the goods are produced.

While Fairtrade International does a lot to promote fair trade, it is not the only organisation that does so. The World Fair Trade Organisation helps to make sure that businesses around the world follow their Ten Principles of Fair Trade, which are similar to the Fairtrade Standards. If a business shows the World Fair Trade Organisation's logo, it means that they are committed to fair trade.

# PROBLEMS WITH FAIR TRADE

Even though most people agree that fair trade is a good idea and could help a lot of people, there are some who believe that making people follow strict rules can actually stop their businesses and farms doing well. Other people think it is unfair to make LED countries use expensive sustainable farming, even if it protects the environment.

Fair trade organisations find it difficult and dangerous to help producers in countries that are fighting a war.

In very poor countries, fair trade organisations can find it very difficult to help, as the governments either can't or won't let them.

This means that even though fair trade money does help the poor countries, the very poorest can get left behind.

# SUPPLY AND DEMAND

To understand the global ecomony, it's important to think about why things are the price they are. Goods usually get cheaper when there are more of them and they become easy to buy. Imagine you are about to start selling lemonade on a beach on a hot day. Before you start selling, everyone on the beach is thirsty. When you start selling, everyone rushes up to buy the lemonade. As you are the only person selling lemonade, you can charge lots of money for it.

Now imagine that five more people turn up and start selling lemonade as well. When the people on the beach can choose who they buy lemonade from, they probably won't buy it from you if the price is very high.

Because of this, everyone on the beach must sell their lemonade at the same low price if they still want to get customers. Supply and demand is important to small economies, like the beach, and also big economies, like the global economy.

# CASE STUDY:
# THE GLOBAL ECONOMIC CRISIS

The Global Economic Crisis of 2008 shows how the economies of different countries are connected. In the 1990's, banks in the U.S.A. were lending people lots of money to buy houses.

People then paid the money back a little bit at a time. This is called a loan. The banks thought that, as long as the economy stayed strong, they would be OK.

WHEN YOU PAY BACK A LOAN, YOU USUALLY HAVE TO PAY BACK MORE MONEY THAN YOU BORROWED. THIS IS HOW THE ORGANISATIONS THAT GIVE OUT LOANS MAKE MONEY.

As lots of people used loans to buy expensive houses, more houses were built, and more loans were given. Too many houses were eventually built – more than people could buy.

At that point, the price of houses in the U.S.A. started to fall – just like the lemonade on the beach. People still had their big loans, but now the houses weren't worth much money anymore.

When people couldn't pay back the loans, the banks and organisations lost lots of money. This meant there was less money in the economy as a whole – lots of things, not just houses, were affected.

When this happens to an economy, and people and businesses have less money than before, it is called an economic crash.

This shows us how economies around the world are all connected. When the U.S.A.'s economy crashed, it caused problems for the people living there, as the everything got more expensive.

But it also caused a global problem, as the U.S.A. stopped buying goods from around the world, so other economies had problems too, and some of them also crashed.

# GET INVOLVED!

## BUY FAIRTRADE

When you are shopping with your family, look for the Fairtrade logo on products like chocolate, coffee, bananas, flowers – even footballs!

These might not be more expensive, but you will know that a fair amount of your money will go to the producers.

## RAISE SOME MONEY

Why not bake some cakes using Fairtrade ingredients, and have a cake sale to raise some money for the Fairtrade foundation?

Or you could have a stall at your school fair with a 'Guess How Many Coffee Beans Are in the Jar' – Fairtrade beans, of course!

# BECOME A FAIRTRADE SCHOOL

Did you know your school can become an official Fairtrade school? Schools can choose to use Fairtrade food in the canteen, or Fairtrade cotton in your uniforms.

Your school can also teach you about Fairtrade, and help to raise money. Then your school can call itself a Fairtrade school. Ask your teacher about how your school can get involved.

Find out more at
www.fairtrade.org.uk

# SPREAD THE WORD

Talking to people can be very powerful. Why not take time to talk to people and help spread the word about Fairtrade. Talk to your teacher about how to get involved. Ask your parents to buy Fairtrade bananas. If you have a cake stall, talk to your customers about what you have found out about Fairtrade. Find out more about where your food comes from, and help people make good choices. By sharing information, we can help make people's lives fairer and better.

# ACTIVITY

**1** Design a Fairtrade snack! Think about all the products we have talked about, and design a delicious snack using fairtrade ingredients.

**2** What is the name of your snack?
What does the packaging look like?
What are the ingredients?
Don't forget the Fairtrade logo!

**3** What countries do your ingredients come from? If you don't know, can you find out?

# GLOSSARY

**agriculture** — the practice of farming, growing crops and raising animals to produce food and other products

**capital city** — the city that is home to a country's government

**citizens** — the people who live in a certain country

**country** — an area with its own citizens and government

**criteria** — a set of standards by which something is judged

**crops** — a plant that is grown on a large scale to produce food or some other product

**more economically developed countries** — countries with a strong economy

**less economically developed countries** — countries with a weaker economy

**employ** — to give work to someone and to pay them for it

**equal** — being the same in quality or status

**exploited** — to use a person in a way that is unfair and unequal

**fertile** — land that is very good for growing crops in

**fossil fuels** — fuels, such as coal, oil and gas, that formed millions of years ago from the remains of animals and plants

**goods** — resources that are transported between different countries

**government** — the group of people with the authority to control and make the laws for a country

**habitats** — the natural homes of different animals and plants

**international** — existing, occurring or travelling between different countries

**isolated** — far away from animals, people or places

**organisations** — an organised group of people with a particular purpose, such as a government or business

**pollute** — make poisonous or dirty by the actions of humans

**ports** — a town or city with access to water, meaning that ships and boats can unload their goods there

**resources** — supplies of money, materials, food or people that can be used to make money

**transport** — move from one place to another using vehicles such as cars, trucks, aeroplanes and boats

**services** — a job that someone is paid to do which does not involve any physical goods being exchanged

# INDEX